WITHDRAWN

An Insider's Guide to

WATER POLO

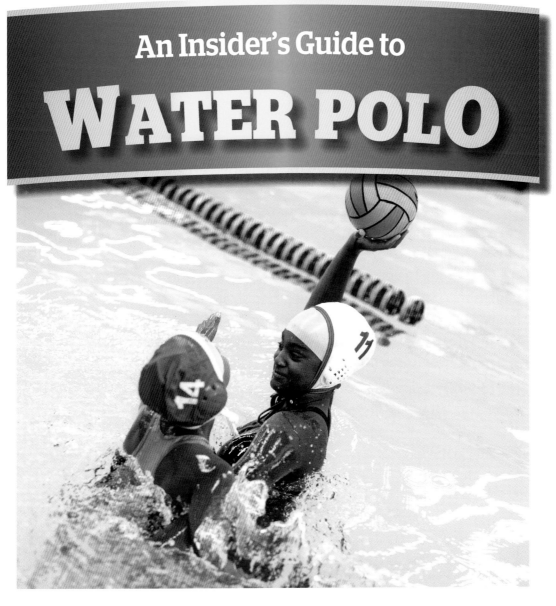

KENNETH ZAHENSKY AND TRACIE EGAN

rosen publishing's
rosen
central®

NEW YORK

Published in 2015 by The Rosen Publishing Group, Inc.
29 East 21st Street, New York, NY 10010

First Edition

Library of Congress Cataloging-in-Publication Data

Zahensky, Kenneth.
An insider's guide to water polo/Kenneth Zahensky and Tracie Egan.
    pages cm.—(Sports tips, techniques, and strategies)
Includes bibliographical references and index.
ISBN 978-1-4777-8085-5 (library bound)
ISBN 978-1-4777-8086-2 (pbk.)
ISBN 978-1-4777-8087-9 (6-pack)
1. Water polo—Juvenile literature. I. Egan, Tracie. II. Title.

GV839.Z34 2015
797.2'52—dc23

2014013508

Manufactured in Malaysia

Metric Conversion Chart			
1 inch	2.54 centimeters 25.4 millimeters	1 cup	250 milliliters
1 foot	30.48 centimeters	1 ounce	28 grams
1 yard	.914 meters	1 fluid ounce	30 milliliters
1 square foot	.093 square meters	1 teaspoon	5 milliliters
1 square mile	2.59 square kilometers	1 tablespoon	15 milliliters
1 ton	.907 metric tons	1 quart	.946 liters
1 pound	454 grams	355 degrees F	180 degrees C
1 mile	1.609 kilometers		

Contents

CHAPTER 1

The Origins of the Game

Water polo is a relatively young game compared with many other sports that have been played for hundreds or even thousands of years. Little is known about the origin of the sport, but it is believed that a Scotsman named William Wilson helped to create water polo in the 1870s. At this time in Great Britain, swimming races were declining in popularity because spectators were becoming bored with the repetitive nature of the sport. It is not as interesting for an audience to watch individuals

William Wilson devised the first official rules for water polo in the 1870s.

compete against time as it is to watch people compete against each other. Swimming clubs in Great Britain began playing a version of "water soccer" in lakes and rivers, even though man-made swimming pools were in existence and were popular by this time. In 1876, at the request of the swimming club he belonged to in Scotland, Wilson drew up a list of rules for the game. The version that Wilson created was not quite like today's game, but it involved elements of tag, diving, and soccer, just like the modern version of water polo.

The game wasn't considered a significant sport at first. Originally, it was thought of as entertainment for audiences attending swimming competitions or for people at seaside resorts. Eventually, the potential of water polo as a popular sport was recognized, and people began working toward a more refined set of rules for the game.

Sports historians often debate about the origin of the name "water polo." Some people believe that the name is derived from another game known as water derby. Water derby was being played as entertainment for spectators at swimming events as well. In this game, men would mount barrels as if they were riding a horse, and often the name of a well-known racehorse would be painted along the side of the barrel. The object of the game was to knock people off the barrels while a hockey-style game was played on the surface of the water. The similarity between the game of polo that's played with real horses and water derby led people to call it aquatic polo or water polo. Water derby never evolved past a simple entertainment, but the name stuck to the game that William Wilson had developed.

In the early forms of the game, people rarely played in swimming pools. Instead, people preferred playing water polo in lakes.

The term "polo" may have been applied to this sport because of the type of ball, an Indian rubber ball, that was used in early versions of the game. *Pulu* is the Hindi word for "ball," but it was mispronounced by the English as "polo." This second theory is probably a more accurate one because there is no documentation of water derby except for some artists' illustrations.

In its formative years, water polo was just a type of aquatic wrestling and the demonstration of a player's strength. There weren't really positions, and the only offensive strategy used was that each player should try to score a goal every chance he got. The more water polo was played, the more thought people put into the rules so that it could be considered a serious sport. In the 1880s, water polo really began to take off, and most of the rules were created within that decade. The rules that were implemented moved the style of play away from rugby and closer to soccer, with the game being less about brute strength and more about speed and technique. The time of play was established, as was the size of the goal cages. The small rubber "pullu" was replaced by a leather soccer ball.

Belgium's water polo team, pictured here, won the silver medal in the 1908 Summer Olympics in London, England. Six players and one goalie make up the team.

The development of the trudgen stroke transformed water polo. The trudgen stroke, a swimming technique, allowed for a faster moving game that was centered a bit more around swimming. In 1888, Archibald Sinclair, the founder of the London Water Polo League, put together a committee to formalize the rules and to add more structure to the game. What the committee came up with was a set of rules that is very similar to those that are used today. In 1891, the game reached an important milestone. That year, England's two most prestigious universities, Oxford and Cambridge, played their first varsity water polo match.

The rugby style of water polo became a hit in the United States.

Around that time, word of the sport spread to America through Englishman John Robinson, a professional swimming instructor who worked at the Boston Athletic Association. Because Robinson was working in America at the time that Sinclair's water polo committee was changing the rules of the sport, Robinson was unaware of those changes and introduced the rugby style of water polo. Rugby is vaguely similar to American football, which is one of the most popular sports in the United States. The American game took on a football feel. This version of water polo, known as "American style," became a huge hit in the United States. In less than ten years, the sport was played in major arenas such as Madison Square Garden, and was drawing crowds of 15,000 during national championships.

American and English Water Polo

The game that Americans call "soccer" is actually called "football" in most other parts of the world. While water polo was still in its early stages of development, the English referred to it as "water football." Those words meant something very different to American athletes, which may have contributed to the early variations between the American and English versions of water polo.

American water polo is now played in some ways like soccer, as it is in England. The early version of the game in America was like rugby, which is very similar to American football.

Goalkeepers in soccer and water polo function in much the same way. They are allowed to catch the ball in an attempt to prevent goals.

The object of water polo still remains trying to score goals.

The rules for American-style water polo were first published in February 1891, in *Harper's Weekly* magazine. Much like the evolution of the game in England, the early American-style water polo differed greatly from the version of the sport that is played today in the United States. In the beginning, American-style water polo was one of the most dangerous sports ever played. Just about any move was legal, including holding another player underwater for long periods of time. In fact, the intensity of the play and the violence of the game is what attracted most spectators to the sport at the time. As water polo spread across the United States, more teams and leagues were developed. Eventually, U.S. teams adopted the "soccer style" of playing water polo, which was then known as the "English rules" game.

Water polo was played at the Summer Olympic Games for the first time in Paris, France, in 1900. This photograph was probably taken during the 1900 Olympics.

When the game was first introduced in the Olympics, it was still quite rough physically. This U.S. team is playing a match during the 1904 Olympics in St. Louis, Missouri.

By the time water polo was introduced in the United States, the exciting new sport had already spread quickly throughout Europe, with the first league being formed in France, followed by Germany, Belgium, and eventually the entire continent. In 1900, the sport of water polo was widespread enough to be added to the program of the Olympic Games.

In fact, water polo was the first team sport to be added to the Olympic program, leading the way for many other sports. The 1900 Olympic Games were played in Paris, France. The Olympic version of water polo did not attract Americans because traveling abroad was expensive and the Olympic version of water polo would be played according to the "English rules."

Two teams play a game of water polo in Spain. The sport spread throughout Europe a lot faster than it did in the United States.

An international water polo board was established in 1929. It consisted of four representatives from England and four representatives from the Fédération Internationale de Natation Amateur (FINA), the worldwide water sports organization founded in 1908. At first, it was basically a British organization, but since then it has developed into an organization that represents all parts of the world. All water polo matches are now played under the rules defined by FINA.

During the development of water polo, it was strictly a men's game. Water polo was believed to be too rigorous for a proper young lady, not to mention that bathing suits, although quite modest in those days, were thought to be far too revealing for them.

But more and more women around the world were becoming suffragists, advocating for the vote and demanding equality in all activities. It was inevitable that women would also want to get in on the fun and exercise of team sports such as water polo. The first documented women's water polo match was held in the Netherlands in 1906.

In 1911, New York's National Women's Lifesaving League formed a swimming and water polo league. The main organizer of the league was Charlotte Epstein, a legal stenographer from the New York area. She also founded the Women's Swimming Association (WSA).

Epstein wanted to introduce women to the sport of water polo to develop strength, teach lifesaving skills, instill confidence, and most important, have fun. The first FINA Women's Water Polo World Cup was played in 1979, but women's water polo was played in the Olympic Games for the first time in 2000—exactly 100 years after the first men's game.

The Trojans of the University of Southern California celebrate their win at the NCAA Women's Water Polo Championship in Boston, Massachusetts.

CHAPTER 2

Playing Techniques and Equipment

People do not need much equipment to play water polo, because it is difficult enough treading water while playing a game with a ball. But the equipment that is required for an official water polo game is divided into two categories: playing equipment (used by the players) and officiating equipment (used by the referees and secretaries).

The Gear

Because the players are immersed in water up to their necks, it's difficult to tell one player from another, or even which team they belong to by the colors or patterns of their bathing suits. Therefore, players are required to

Two teams (one wearing green numbered caps, the other white numbered caps) compete in a water polo championship. The goalkeeper, who usually wears a red cap with the number 1, blocks the other team's shots.

wear swimming caps that are numbered. One team wears light-colored caps, while the other team wears a dark color. Each goalie wears a red cap with the number 1 on it.

Though the ball used in water polo games has evolved over the years, it is very similar to a soccer ball today. It is round, and it must be fully inflated. If the ball is not fully inflated, it has the potential to be hazardous, as it will bounce swiftly off the water. The circumference measures between 25 and 28 inches. Its weight is between 14 and 16 ounces.

The rectangular water polo pool is generally 82 feet by 66 feet. It should be between 6.5 and 26 feet deep—the deeper the better. Players are supposed to tread water, not walk on the bottom of the pool.

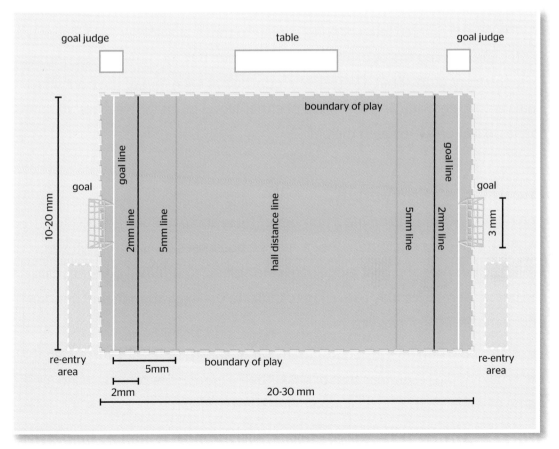

This diagram shows the standard dimensions of a water polo pool.

A regulation water polo pool is laid out, ready for play.
The diagram on the previous page specifies the dimensions.

The pool is divided into sections, similar to those of a soccer field. There is a center line dividing the pool into two halves. Each half has lines measuring out from the front of the goal. There is one goal box at each end of the pool. The goals are 10 feet wide and are made of either wood or metal. Nets are attached to the goal in order to catch the ball.

The Referee's Equipment

The rules of water polo define a number of fouls and penalties, so the most important piece of equipment that a referee possesses is his or her whistle. While the referees and goal judge use hand signals to signify a different call, the game secretaries may use a flag to indicate the expiration of foul periods and game reentry of players.

Water polo borrows aspects of many other sports, so it's not surprising that the timekeeping resembles that of basketball. There are two clocks used for a game of water polo, as in basketball. One clock, called the shot clock, indicates how much time remains for the offense to shoot the ball into the goal, while the other indicates the time remaining in a quarter.

Water polo referees, who usually dress in white, signal fouls by blowing the whistle and making hand signals. Referees also have total control of the game and monitor players' actions.

The Techniques

Playing techniques for water polo are as important as the rules of the game. Many skills are required of a player, the most obvious one being the ability to swim. Because swimming uses every muscle in the body and is extremely exhausting, an athlete must be in top shape to swim or tread water for an entire game of water polo. The best swimming position for the game is, obviously, one where the player can see what is going on. Water polo players do not use the usual competitive swimming style, with the body as horizontal as possible and the head in the water. Instead, they use a style in which their head is above the water, much like the one lifeguards use.

Goalies are the only members of the team who are allowed to touch the ball with both hands. Goalies need to be alert and judge when the ball will reach the goal to block it successfully.

Another important skill in water polo that is vital to catching, passing, or shooting the ball is treading water. While treading water, the player is in a vertical (upright) position, with the head and preferably the shoulders above the water. The legs are constantly kicking in what's known as an eggbeater kick, where the legs move alternately, resembling a kitchen eggbeater. The arms are used to maintain balance, but when the arms are needed for handling the ball, the legs are required to work overtime in order for the player's body to maintain a vertical position.

Swimming and treading water are the most basic skills required of a water polo player. But to score goals, it is also necessary for a player to be a competent ball handler. Players who hold the ball with as little tension as possible are the best handlers.

For this player to make a lob shot into the goal, he has to kick up high and hard so that his body is raised up, providing more power to his arm.

The ball is never held in the flat of the hand. It is always held partially in the palm and partially on the fingers. The fingers must remain relaxed, while the arm remains bent, forming a right angle at the elbow. When throwing the ball, the arm rotates, drawing the ball back. The ball is held high from the surface of the water. The arm then swings forward, while the body faces the spot that the player intends to pass to. The legs should still be "egg beating" while the free arm is maintaining balance.

Controlling the ball while swimming is quite a difficult task. It is important for the player to adhere to established techniques in order to be a better handler and dribbler. In water polo, dribbling is when a player swims with the ball. Dribbling achieved through a "crawl" stroke, where the player moves forward in the water with his or her head up, while stroking with the arms. A wave created by the chest carries the ball. The ball moves with the wave as the player moves forward. To change directions when dribbling, the player can nudge the ball with the inside of his or her arms while turning the body.

In water polo, there are "wet" passes and "dry" passes. Wet passes are when the ball hits the water first before reaching one's teammate. Dry passes are when the ball is passed directly from player to player without touching the water. It is much more difficult to successfully execute a dry pass, as it is difficult enough to tread water and see everything going on during the game. Most passes made are wet passes because they are easier to manage. A wet pass, if properly executed, tends to put the ball in the water right in front of your teammate. A dry pass may require your teammate to rise out of the water at just the right moment to catch the ball.

Passing the ball to other players is important for victory, but games could not be won without the skill of shot-taking. Many players view shooting as the most important technique, but it's also the skill that must be practiced most. To master an accurate shot, it is important to have a good eye and a strong wrist.

The ball is not held while the player is moving.
It is dribbled with the help of the waves created by the chest.

This goalie looks helplessly at the lob shot that just cost him a goal.
Lob shots arch over the goalie's head and land in the goal.

A goal can be taken by a number of different shots. The lob shot, for example, is a deceptive, high arching shot that is intended to pass over the goalie and under the crossbar of the goal. Another type of shot is the sling shot. It resembles that of a discus thrower: the ball is thrown using a straight arm that is parallel to the water's surface and moving with a low sweep over the water. Finally, the push shot is a straightforward, pushing maneuver that is meant to look like a natural swimming stroke. The various shots have their advantages and disadvantages, which make them important to master during practice drills.

Obviously, shooting, passing, and dribbling are the main techniques for offensive play in water polo. But the techniques of defensive play are just as essential. The two major features of defensive play are marking and tackling. Both are used to break up the offense. Water polo players physically interact with one another, using their bodies to block the ball or other players, which makes water polo a contact sport. Marking occurs when a defensive player chooses an offensive player to guard. Tackling occurs when a defensive player holds, pulls, or pushes down an offensive player, usually when the offensive player is holding the ball. Tackling is legal in water polo, as long as it is carried out in a manner that will not cause injury.

Of course, skill is a plus in any sport, but an athlete cannot rely solely on natural ability. Knowing about the various techniques of water polo can help improve your game—but practice makes perfect.

The defense tries to take possession of the ball by tackling the offense.

CHAPTER 3

How to Play the Game

It can be confusing to watch water polo if you do not know the rules. The game is loud and fast paced, with a lot of motion and splashing.

Water polo is a fast-paced game that requires great speed and stamina. Shooting and passing under pressure, and being able to communicate plays to teammates are other necessary skills.

The whistle of the referee always seems to be in use, although game play remains continuous, even when a foul or penalty is called. Constant action is essential in water polo, since it was initially intended to be a spectator sport. So the rules have been devised with the audience in mind, to keep the action going.

The object of water polo, as with most ball sports, is to score points by getting the ball into the opponent's goal. The team with the most points at the end of the game is the victor. The ball is advanced on the court, or pool,

by throwing it or swimming with it. One of the fundamental rules of water polo is that no player other than the goalie may use both hands at the same time when handling the ball. Players are also not permitted to strike a water polo ball with a closed fist, in the way that a volleyball player spikes a ball, although they are allowed to use other body parts to advance the ball or to take a shot on the goal.

A game of water polo is divided into four quarters, each quarter lasting seven minutes. As in basketball, when the offensive team is on the opponent's side of the pool, they have a limited amount of time to take a shot at the goal. A score does not have to occur, but a shot must be attempted. If a shot is not attempted in the thirty-five-second time period, the offense will lose possession of the ball.

There are lines marked on each half of the pool. Each line has its own purpose. The two-meter line is located two meters in front of the goal. The offensive team cannot pass this line unless they are holding the ball or if the ball is in front of them. The four-meter line is located four meters in front of the goal. An offensive player may be awarded a penalty shot if he or she is in possession of the ball and is fouled in the area between the goal and the four-meter line. Seven meters in front of

At the start of each quarter, all players swim quickly toward
the center line to try to gain possession of the ball.

the goal is the seven-meter line. When a foul is committed against an offensive player beyond this line, the player may take a free throw or a direct shot into the goal. The center line is what it sounds like—it is located in the center of the water polo field. At the start of each quarter, the ball is placed on the center line. Each team then races from its own goal line, swimming at top speed, to gain possession of the ball. This action is known as the sprint. Whichever side the ball is then taken over to is called the strong side, while the side without the ball is called the weak side. After a goal is scored, the players take positions anywhere within their respective fields of play.

In many sports, fouls are considered a hindrance to play by both the offense and the defense, and are typically avoided. However, in water polo, as in basketball, fouls are part of an offensive team's strategy. The offense will typically try to get the defense to commit fouls because the free throws and penalty shots that can be awarded provide the best opportunity to score a goal.

There are three types of fouls in water polo: ordinary, exclusion, and penalty fouls. Ordinary fouls are called for minor offenses that include touching the ball with two hands, taking the ball underwater, wasting time, or obstructing an offensive player without the ball. Pushing, failing to advance the ball, or failing to take a shot at the goal within the thirty-five-second time limit are the other ordinary fouls.

Intentional splashing and dunking are major fouls in water polo. The defense is careful to tackle without committing a foul.

The Four Quarters

In a water polo game, there are four quarters of play, each not longer than seven minutes. The entire game consists of only twenty-eight minutes of play. For this reason, the rules are designed to keep the game going as continuously and as quickly as possible. Stalling, or wasting time, is a common reason for calling an ordinary foul.

The player with the ball must turn away from an opponent while picking up the ball, otherwise the opponent might knock the ball out of his or her hand.

When a referee calls an ordinary foul, possession of the ball is given over to the opposing team at the location of the foul. If an ordinary foul is called on the defense between the two-meter line and the goal, the offense is automatically awarded a free throw at the goal. The free throw must be taken within three seconds, and if the ball is not put into play within three seconds, possession of the ball is awarded to the defense.

Exclusion fouls are for more serious infractions, including kicking or striking an opponent with intent to injure, interfering with a free throw, splashing, and misconduct such as foul language, violent behavior, or disrespecting referees.

When an exclusion foul is called, the opposing team is awarded a free throw, while the player who has committed the foul is temporarily removed from the game. The player is sent to the reentry area, which is located near the team's bench at the side of the pool. He or she is not allowed to return to the game until twenty seconds of actual game play has occurred, possession of the ball changes, or a goal has been scored. If a player commits three exclusion fouls in a game, he or she is removed from the game completely.

One of the most common formations used during water polo games is shown here. The attacking team (in white) has four players positioned on two meters, and two players positioned on four meters. The five outfield defending players (in blue) try to block shots and prevent a goal.

Because an exclusion foul leaves a team with one fewer player, goals are more easily scored by the opposing team. A popular strategy in water polo is to provoke a player of the opposing team into committing an exclusion foul, because attacking the goal with a one-man advantage will more likely result in a score. During an exclusion, a team will switch from marking into a zone defense. When a player guards an area of the water rather than another player, it is called zone defense.

The most serious infractions are penalty fouls. They are called when a defending player commits any foul that obstructs a likely score, when a defending player commits an act of brutality within the four-meter area, or when the coach of the team not in possession of the ball requests a time-out.

When a penalty foul is called on a player, the opposing team is awarded a penalty throw. A penalty throw is a direct shot on the goal and is thrown by the person that the foul was committed against.

For each of these fouls—ordinary, exclusion, and penalty—the referee can award throws to the offense as he or she

The defensive player in the blue cap tries to knock down the ball from the offensive player's possession. This type of defense is legal in water polo.

sees fit. There are several different types of throws, each with its own style and purpose. When a free throw is awarded to the offense, the defense may not block or interfere with the throw in any manner. If they do, another foul will be called. A corner throw is a kind of free throw awarded to the offense when the defense touches the ball before it crosses the defensive goal line, outside of the goalposts. The offensive team will then throw the ball back into play from the side of the two-meter line. Another type of throw is a neutral throw. This is also referred to as a face-off. Face-offs are awarded when two players, one from offense and one from defense, commit a foul at the same time. The referee will blow his or her whistle and drop the ball between the players during a face-off.

Other than being removed from the game by an exclusion foul, a player is not allowed to leave the water unless it is during an interval, or time between quarters, or when a referee gives a player permission (usually in the case of an emergency). In these cases, a substitute is allowed to enter the game.

Not a Foul!

Unlike in basketball, in water polo, the player holding the ball cannot be fouled. A player is considered to be holding the ball if it is in his or her hand or if it is floating on the water with the player's hand on top of it. A player is not considered to be holding the ball if he or she is dribbling, that is, swimming with the ball cradled in the water near the chest. It is legal to grab, push, hold, or dunk the holder of the ball. These actions make water polo exceptionally exciting, with a slight resemblance to rugby.

This player is not considered to be holding the ball because
it is neither in his hand nor is his hand on top of it.

The Officials

A water polo referee has a hard job. The game is quick moving, and fouls are constantly being committed. The referee must have a quick eye and make fast judgments about which fouls should be called. Because infractions are such a large part of the strategy of water polo, a referee employs what is known as the advantage rule. This principle is when a referee may refrain from calling a foul if he or she feels that making that call would give the advantage to the defense.

There are other officials in water polo who help the referee. There are two goal judges, one on each side of the pool. Their job is to indicate whether or not a goal has been scored. There are also two secretaries, who manage the game

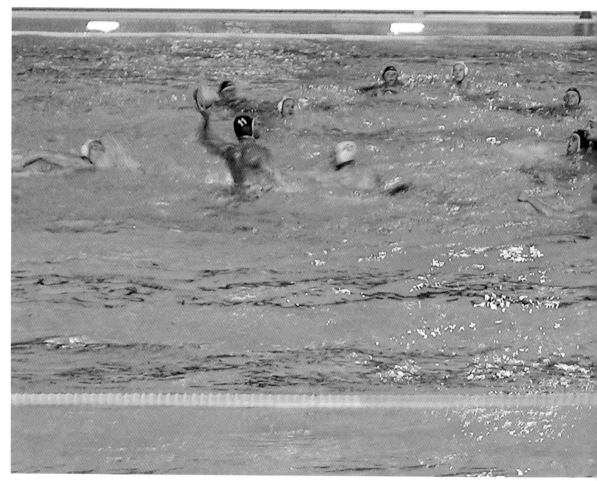

The quickness of water polo requires referees to have a keen eye and fast reflexes. Referees cannot afford to take their eye off the ball for even a second.

clocks, record all serious fouls committed by players, and signal when a third exclusion or penalty foul has been made, to help determine if a player needs to be removed from the game.

Because water polo is such a young sport and the rules have been modified so many times over the years, it is hard for referees to keep up. To deal with the problems that referees encounter, many countries have formed organizations for referees to help them perform their job. This assistance is partly the result of complaints and threats from the Olympic committee to have the game erased from the Olympic program if the standards of refereeing do not improve. Standardized tests regarding the rules of the game and how to

call fouls are issued to referees through these organizations. However, criticism of water polo referees is still common. Many believe that the quality of players and coaches has improved since the invention of the game but the quality of the referees has not.

To combat this problem, FINA offers a water polo referee school. The goal of the referee school is to increase the number as well as the quality of referees and to create uniform interpretations and applications of the rules of water polo. Only certified graduates of the FINA referee school may be selected for FINA-sanctioned competitions. In order to continue as a FINA water polo referee, a FINA-certified referee must be re-examined and updated on changing rules every two years.

CHAPTER 4

Player Positions and Coaches

There are thirteen players on most water polo teams, but only seven players (including the goalkeeper) are allowed to be in the pool at one time. Team members who are sitting out the game must remain on the team bench and are not allowed to get up, except during a game interval. Because water polo is a game of thought and strategy as well as action, the positions of the players are important. Each player has a certain position in the pool when it comes to defense and offense. The positions of water polo are similar to those in basketball and soccer.

The defense is on alert, trying to block the offense's attempt at a goal.

Drivers are similar to guards in basketball. Drivers look for scoring opportunities for themselves and other team members. They specialize in driving skills, which include quick-shooting techniques, exceptional hand-eye coordination, and an extremely fast swimming technique. Though drivers are mainly offensive players, they get involved in defensive play sometimes.

Another offensive player is the center forward. A center forward positions himself or herself in front of the opponent's goal, between the two-meter and four-meter lines. This area is known as the hole. The center forward is sometimes called the hole man, and the shots that he or she takes are called hole shots. It's beneficial for the center forward to be a large player. A center

The center forward attempts a shot while the defensive players try to stop him.

forward must have extraordinary leg strength and passing abilities. He or she must also be skilled at shot-taking, as he or she will be trying to score for most of the game. The position of center forward is similar to basketball's center position in that this player awaits a pass that will get him or her close to the goal for a shot. Center forwards are always heavily guarded by the defense.

More and more teams are starting to train utility players. Utility players' positions can't be clearly defined, as they play many roles in the water. Similar to halfbacks in soccer, utility players are both offensive and defensive players. They are the strongest shooters on the team and are in constant play, moving to wherever the ball may be, but mostly searching out opportunities to score goals.

The main line of defense in water polo is the two-meter defenders. The two-meter defenders are in charge of guarding the center forwards, or hole men. The most useful quality in a two-meter defender is agility, as he or she will have to block passes constantly. The maximum number of fouls are committed by the two-meter defenders, so they must take care not to commit more than three, as they run the risk of being removed from the game. The two-meter defender position is perhaps the most physically strenuous of all the positions in water polo. Most of the action is happening under the water, as the defender is usually pulling at the center forward, trying to hold him or her back from receiving passes or scoring. Two-meter defenders are the last line of defense before the goalies.

The two-meter defenders and the goalie failed to deflect
the ball, resulting in a goal for the offense.

Goalies are the only players who are allowed to use both hands at once to handle the ball or to punch it with a closed fist, as long as they are within the four-meter line. The goalkeeper's main duty is to patrol the area between the goalposts and to make saves that will prevent scores. Goalies are not permitted to go beyond the center line, but they are allowed to take shots on an opponent's goal, so long as it's done from their half of the pool.

The Coach: The Team's Backbone

The techniques and physical demands of water polo are difficult to master and require an intense amount of training and organization. For these reasons the role of coaching is a crucial one. The duties of a water polo coach are far-reaching. Not only are coaches in charge of instructing their players, but they need to be effective team managers. A coach should coordinate swimming training, ball skills, drills, land conditioning (when a team trains out of the pool),

Ratko Rudić is the most successful coach in the history of water polo.
He coached the Croatian team to an Olympic gold in 2012.
He won a total of 36 medals as a coach at major events,
including three Olympic golds.

and strategies. To accomplish these tasks, coaches must make use of not only athletic but also scientific, technical, and administrative resources. Many coaches study their craft through different manuals that are available from such organizations as the USA Water Polo Coaches' Association. With constant evolution of the drills and exercises employed to maximize a player's skills, coaches recognize that they need to stay current in order to lead their team to victory.

The USA Water Polo Coaches' Association has an outlined code of ethics for water polo coaches. The USA Water Polo Coaches' Association expects its coaches to have integrity. It expects coaches to be honest and fair. It also asks for professional responsibility from coaches. Most important, the USA Water Polo Coaches' Association requests that coaches respect the officials and the players, and always put the welfare of the players before everything.

A coach's responsibility goes beyond ensuring that players are prepared. At matches, coaches also give pep talks to boost the morale of the players and give them strategies and advice.

A good coach can recognize when a player is sick or tired. It is vital for coaches and players to have a strong working relationship. The coach is essentially a member of the team, and as a team, the best road toward victory is for team members to work together.

Because of the rigor and strength required of a water polo player, playing the game is obviously not for everybody, which may be the reason why the sport is not more popular than it is now. But participants in the sport are aware of this drawback and are working to change it. Each year, the association USA Water Polo holds a meeting to discuss the future of the sport. Usually, the meetings are focused on the Olympics, but the association also works to promote interest in the sport on other amateur and professional levels.

However, almost anybody can enjoy being a spectator. Water polo was, after all, invented as a spectator sport. It is not that common to catch a water polo match on television, but there are plenty of competitions and tournaments that take place on many levels, including high school, college, and international venues, and even local clubs.

Not Playing Fair

Water polo players are extremely competitive and therefore will do anything to increase their performance in a game. Many players will shave their body hair to cut down on resistance in the water. Sometimes, players will try to put grease or oil on their bodies to increase their speed in the water. However, the player who applies these products to his or her body will usually have a substitution play instead, because these actions are not legal.

The "Blood in the Water" Match

A match that took place during the 1956 Summer Olympics, held in Melbourne, Australia, went down in history as one of the most famous water polo matches of all time. As the Hungarian athletes departed for Melbourne, a Soviet army, 200,000 strong, suppressed a smaller army of anti-communists in Budapest. Many of the Hungarian athletes were uncertain about whether they would ever return home and said their final farewells to their loved ones.

The Soviet Union and Hungary then faced off in a semi-final water polo match in Melbourne. Many Hungarians who were then living in Australia filled the stands to cheer on their homeland team. News reports from Hungary had described the brutality that the people there were suffering under Soviet control. The Hungarian water polo team felt the only way to fight back was to beat the Soviet team.

Hungary's Dezso Gyarmati, who is considered to be the greatest water polo player of all time by some experts today, hit his Soviet defender when he scored the first goal. Another Hungarian star,

GYARMATI
DEZSŐ
VIZILABDA
1964

A statue of legendary player Deszo Gyarmati stands in Budapest, Hungary. Gyarmati died on August 18, 2013.

Ervin Zador, was pummeled by a Russian player after he scored two goals. He suffered a deep gash under his right eye. The photograph of the bleeding Zador was published in newspapers worldwide. The referee ended the match with less than a minute left. The pool had turned red with blood and there was fear that the battle would spread to the stands. Hungary, however, won the match against the Soviets 4-0, and then went on to win the championship by defeating Yugoslavia.

In June 2002, twelve players from both teams reunited in Budapest and reflected on the bloody match. Zador, who was one of the twelve players at the reunion, stated, "It should be clear that we never had any ill feelings toward the Russian people. It was just a match at the wrong time and the wrong place." A Russian player also admitted at the reunion that, though his team was under immense pressure, Hungary would have won in any case, because it was the better team.

Glossary

advantage rule The referee's option not to declare a foul, if it is his or her judgment that doing so would be an advantage to the offender's team. This option speeds up the game and can result in more scoring.

brutality An exclusion foul that includes deliberately attacking an opponent or making any movements that are intended to endanger another player.

competent Possessing the necessary knowledge, logic, or skill to do something successfully.

dribble To move and control the ball while swimming the crawl stroke.

drivers Field players who specialize in swimming quickly toward the goal and shooting the ball well.

infraction A violation of rules.

integrity The quality of being honest and fair.

interval A pause or break that takes place during a game. This break happens in water polo in between quarters and at halftime.

potential Having the ability to develop into something in the future.

pummel To beat with fists.

rigorous Extremely thorough and careful.

substitution The act of replacing one person for another; someone that is substituted for another.

treading A cyclical movement of legs used by water polo players to remain upright in deep water.

trudgen stroke A crawl variation that uses alternating overarm strokes with a scissors kick, named for J. Arthur Trudgen, a famous British swimming instructor who was introduced to the swimming stroke in South America in the 1870s. In water polo, it enables quick passes, stops, starts, and turns.

For More Information

American Water Polo
320 West 5th Street
Bridgeport, PA 19405
(610) 277-6787
Website: http://www.
americanwaterpolo.org/

Collegiate Water Polo Association
320 W. 5th Street
Bridgeport, PA 19405
(610) 277-6787
Website: http://www.
collegiatewaterpolo.org/splash/index

FINA World League
Av. De l'Avant—Poste 4
1005 Lausanne
Switzerland
Website: http://fina.org

Los Angeles Water Polo Club
23679 Calabasas Rd #517
Calabasas, CA 91302
(818) 495-4186
Website: http://www.
losangeleswaterpolo.com/#wrapper
National Collegiate Athletic Association

National Collegiate Athletic Association
(NCAA)
700 W. Washington Street
P.O. Box 6222
Indianapolis, IN 46206
(317) 917-6222
Website: http://www.ncaa.org

SOCAL Water Polo
P.O. Box 1996
Tustin, CA
(714) 269-0385
Website: http://www.socalwaterpolo.
org/w/index.cfm

USA Water Polo, Inc.
2124 Main Street
Suite 240
Huntington Beach, CA 92648
(714) 500-5445
Website: http://www.usawaterpolo.org

Websites
Because of the changing nature of
Internet links, the Rosen Publishing has
developed an online list of websites
related to the subject of this book.
 This site is updated regularly. Please
use this link to access the list:

http://www.rosenlinks.com/STTS/
WPolo

For Further Reading

Fury, David. *Johnny Weissmuller: Twice the Hero*. Minneapolis, MN: Artist's Press, 2013.

Goldblatt, David. *The Ball Is Round: A Global History of Soccer*. New York, NY: Riverhead Books, 2008.

Guzman, Ruben. *The Swimming Drill Book*. Champaign, IL: Human Kinetics, 2007.

Hardman, Lizabeth. *Swimming (Science Behind Sports)*. Farmington Hills, MI: Lucent Books, 2011.

Henry, William. *Water Polo: A Brief History, Rules of the Game and Instructions on How to Play*. London, UK: Malinowski Press, 2010.

Hines, Chuck. *Water Polo the Y's Way*. Bloomington, IN: Author House, 2008.

Lucerno, Blyth. *100 Best Swimming Drills*. London, UK: Meyer and Meyer Sport, 2011.

McLeod, Ian. *Swimming Anatomy*. Champaign, IL: Human Kinetics, 2009.

Sundstrom, Gus. *Water Polo*. Wellington, NZ: Ulan Press, 2012.

Bibliography

De Mestre, Neville. *Water Polo: Techniques and Tactics*. Sydney, AU: Angus and Robertson, 1972.

Hale, Ralph W., ed. *The Complete Book of Water Polo: The U.S. Olympic Water Polo Team's Manual for Conditioning, Strategy, Tactics, and Rules*. New York, NY: Simon & Schuster, 1986.

Lambert, Arthur F. *The Technique of Water Polo: A Text for Player and Coach*. North Hollywood, CA: Swimming World, 1969.

Smith, James R. *Playing and Coaching Water Polo*. Los Angeles, CA: W. F. Lewis, 1948.

Index

Index

About the Authors

Kenneth Zahensky is long-time fan of U.S. water polo and lives in Westchester, New York. He has played on two water polo club teams in New York throughout the years.

Tracie Egan is a writer who lives in Brooklyn, New York.

Photo Credits

The photographs in this book are used by permission and through the courtesy of: Getty Images, 1; back cover: © Haslam Photography/shutterstock.com; © Tomas Fritz/shutterstock.com; ©Baronb/shutterstock.com; © aquariagirl1970/shutterstock.com; © Ryanjo/commons.wikimedia.org; © DeanHarty/shutterstock.com; © Micha Klootwijk/shutterstock.com; © File Upload Bot (Magnus Manske)/commons.wikimedia.org, 3, 8; © Ryanjo/File Upload Bot (Magnus Manske)/commons.wikimedia.org, 4, 21, 39; © Darwinius/commons.wikimedia.org, 5; © Papifef/commons.wikimedia.org, 6; © JZCL/commons.wikimedia.org, 7; © mooinblack/Shutterstock.com, 8; © muratart/Shutterstock.com, 8; © FreeMO/commons.wikimedia.org, 9; © Voyager/commons.wikimedia.org, 10; © Juan Fernández/File Upload Bot (Magnus Manske)/commons.wikimedia.org, 11; © Mike Broglio/Shutterstock.com, 12, 13; © Pukhov Konstantin/Shutterstock.com, 14; © Joe Belanger/Shutterstock.com, 16; © muzsy/Shutterstock.com, 17, 20, 27, 31; © Ryanjo/commons.wikimedia.org, 18, 19; © Ryanjo/Valepert/commons.wikimedia.org, 22; © Иван Ђурчић/File Upload Bot (Magnus Manske)/ commons.wikimedia.org, © Getty Images, 23; 24, 25; © Zorro2212/commons.wikimedia.org, 26; © Kris Kras Foto/G-Staaf/commons.wikimedia.org, 28; © Prisonblues /Siebrand/commons.wikimedia.org, 29; © Lario Tus/Shutterstock.com, 30; © Sebjarod/commons.wikimedia.org, 32, 33; © Denis Radovanovic/Shutterstock.com, 34; © Natursports/Shutterstock.com, 35, 38; © luca85/Shutterstock.com, 36; © SpeedyGonsales/commons.wikimedia.org, 37; © Fmvh/commons.wikimedia.org, 40.